Peace Trumps Place:
A Collection of Poems

Abby Wright Gonzalez

BookLeaf Publishing

India | USA | UK

Presentation by *BookLeaf Publishing*

Web: www.bookleafpub.com

E-mail: info@bookleafpub.com

ISBN: 9789358313390

First edition 2024

DEDICATION

To my children,

I'm so proud to be your mother.

xoxo,

Mama

ACKNOWLEDGEMENT

First and foremost, I would like to express my gratitude to my husband, Carlos and our children, who have always been my biggest supporters. Their unconditional love and unwavering belief in me have given me the confidence to pursue my dreams.

I would also like to thank my friends, Donna and Tina, who have provided me with invaluable feedback and support throughout this journey. Our conversations have always been a constant source of inspiration. Regardless of the time apart, we always pick up right where we left off.

Finally, to my readers, thank you for taking the time to engage with my work. Your support and feedback mean more to me than you can imagine.

Thank you all for being a part of this journey with me. I am truly grateful for your love and support.

PREFACE

My dear reader,
I invite you to embark on a journey with me.
Through the pages of my poetry,
we'll explore what it means to be:
An adopted child, a traveler,
and a seeker of self-discovery.
In the language of poetry,
let us embark on this odyssey.

Duality

Two worlds that I've lived within remain in view,
Two worlds I've emerged from, I overgrew;
Those worlds appear smaller when in rearview.

Thoughts pervade my mind but never breakthrough,
The love I needed, I will now pass onto
Two worlds that I've lived within remain in view.

Continue to swim, never cease pursuit.
Two worlds and now I move towards my truth,
Those worlds appear smaller when in rearview.

You'd think within depths that risks will ensue,
The strength I need is in my queue.
Two worlds that I've lived within remain in view.

Keep swimming in the depths, waters dark blue,
The actions I make will not misconstrue;
Those worlds appear smaller when in rearview.

Tell the thoughts to slow down, then bid adieu,
Curse, bless, me now with musings impromptu.
Two worlds that I've lived that remain in view.
Those worlds appear smaller when in rearview.

Everything Relates

In every moment
A connection can be found
Everything relates

From the smallest grain
To the vast expanse of space
All is intertwined

A single moment
Affects the course of our lives
Interwoven fates

The beating of hearts
The rhythm of the seasons
Nature's symphony

So remember this
In this vast and wondrous world
Everything relates.

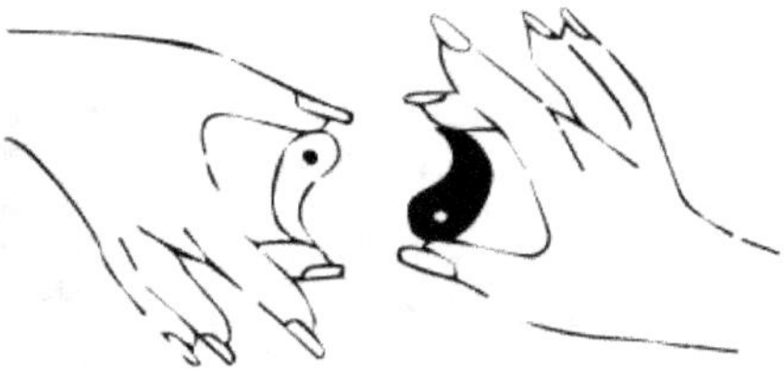

Duality of Adoption

In the world of adoption, there's a duality
Of place and peace, which reigns supreme?
Does where you're from dictate your reality?

For some, their past is full of brutality
Their present home a loving team
In the world of adoption, there's a duality

Others feel a sense of loyalty
To the place of birth, their lifelong scene
Does where you're from dictate your reality?

But what if we focus on the quality
Of life, rather than the place we dream
In the world of adoption, there's a duality

For children, love should be the priority
Regardless of country or regime
Does where you're from dictate your reality?

So let's embrace the mentality
That peace trumps place, like a cherished theme
In the world of adoption, there's a duality
But where there's love, reality is a possibility.

Does Where You're from Dictate Your Reality?

Does where you're from dictate your reality?
Is your fate predetermined by your roots?
Does your past determine where you'll go?
Or can you break free from your history?
Can you rise above the labels and stereotypes?
Can you create your own destiny?

Some say that where you're born
determines your destiny,
That your surroundings shape your reality,
That you'll always be judged by the stereotypes,
That you'll never escape
the shadow of your roots.
But is it possible to rewrite your history,
To chart a new path, to change where you go?

It's not easy
to break free and decide where you'll go,
To take control of your own destiny,
To leave behind the weight of your history,
And create a new reality,
To grow beyond the confines of your roots,
And shatter the mold of stereotypes.

It takes strength
to challenge the stereotypes,
To refuse to be limited by where you're from,
To dig deep and find the courage to uproot
Yourself from the familiar and choose
your own destiny,
To create a life that reflects your reality,
And to not be defined by your history.

In the end,
it's up to you to make your own history,
To prove the world wrong about the stereotypes,
To create a reality that reflects who you are,
To show that where you're from doesn't
determine where you'll go,
And that you have the power to shape
your own destiny,
To grow beyond your roots, and to be free.

Peace Trumps Place

In a world where borders reign
And nations fight for pride and space
We must remember, peace trumps place

The lust for power is often insane
And the cost of war we cannot face
In a world where borders reign

Let us strive for unity, not disdain
And work towards a harmonious embrace
We must remember, peace trumps place

Our differences should not be a chain
But instead a tapestry of grace
In a world where borders reign

Let us break free from this strain
And strive for a world without a trace
We must remember, peace trumps place

For in the end, what will we gain?
If we're in a constant race
In a world where borders reign
We must remember, peace trumps place.

Pine Island Haikus

The sky a canvas
Colors blend, pink to orange
Pine Island Sunset

Sandcastles arise,
Memories of childhood past,
Joyful innocence.

A day at the beach
Simple pleasures bring us joy
Memories to keep

Pine Island water,
Warm waters of the Gulf stream,
Inviting, refreshing.

Sandcastles tower high
Built with care and childlike glee
Floating dock sways slow

The beauty of life,
Glimpses of paradise found,
Forever cherished.

Find the People
Who are on Your Side

When life feels like a lonely ride,
And all hope seems lost in the tide,
Find the people who are on your side.

In times of darkness, they provide
A light to guide you through the night,
When life feels like a lonely ride.

They lift you up when you're down and tired,
And give you strength to fight the fight,
Find the people who are on your side.

Their love and support won't be denied,
They'll stand with you no matter the strife,
When life feels like a lonely ride.

Look far and wide with open eyes,
Remind yourself to never hide,
Find the people who are on your side.

With them, you'll never need to hide,
Or worry about being denied.
When life feels like a lonely ride,
Find the people who are on your side.

A Journey Sought

In the moments of adventure and discovery,
The thrill of traveling is hard to resist,
Roaming far and wide, seeing new places,
It opens up a world of creative thought,
Stirring the imagination and inspiring art,
A life of wonder and excitement sought.

But the journey is not always forethought,
It can be a struggle, a test of discovery,
A chance to explore and create art,
To find beauty in the mundane, to resist
The temptation to give up creative thought,
And instead find inspiration
in unexpected places.

Like a needle and thread, places
Are woven together, a tapestry of knots,
A patchwork of memories and thoughts,
A journey of self-discovery,
A chance to grow, to learn, to resist
The urge to stagnate and forego the art.

Traveling and creating art,
They are two sides of the same coin, two places
Where the mind can roam free, and resist
The shackles of the mundane, a blind spot,,
A journey of self-discovery,
A chance to explore the depths
of creative thought.

So let us embrace the power of creative thought,
And let our art be a reflection of our travels,
A testament to our journey of self-discovery,
A tribute to the places we have been
and the places
We will go within the life we've got,
A chance to break free and resist.

In the moments of adventure and discovery,
Traveling and creative thought go hand in hand,
A journey well-sought, no longer resist.
And find beauty in unexpected places,
create art.

Our Kitchen Slow Dance

Synchronicity in the kitchen,
A couple cooks side by side,
A symphony of flavors

Synchronicity in the kitchen,
A dance of knives and pots,
Ingredients mingle in harmony.

Synchronicity in the kitchen,
Aromas filling the air,
Balanced flavors dance.

Synchronicity in the kitchen,
Food's duality delights,
Tango on the tongue.

One dish, two flavors collide,
Sweet meets savory in one bite.

Chaos Reigns

My girl,
Ever curious,
Eager to learn and explore,
Inquisitive mind seeking truth,
My joy.

My boy,
Blessed with an extra chromosome,
A heart of gold,
A smile that brightens any day,
My sunshine.

My boy,
Strong-willed and bold,
Chasing his dreams with fervor,
Confidently taking on the world,
My hero.

Three kids,
Chaos reigns
Bouncing off the walls
Laughter fills the air, as they
Exhaust me.

Coffee Mid-Day

No, you can't watch the TV,
No, I can't look while I drive
The dog ate the trash,
Someone passed gas,
Just trying to keep y'all alive.

With chaos our house is ornate,
I must learn to delegate,
My mind erases,
when missing those faces,
It's time that I re-caffeinate.

Yes, I'd love snuggles at bedtime
Yes, a family of five.
Volunteer at school
They say "your mom's cool"
Today is a day that we thrive.

Family Road Trip

As we hit the open road, my mind begins to wander. The passing scenery inspires so many thoughts and emotions. The winding roads and sprawling landscapes seem to stretch out before us, inviting me to explore the unknown.

As the sun sets over the horizon, I can't help but reflect on the journey so far. The memories we've made along the way are etched into my mind forever. From the laughter-filled car rides to the quiet moments of reflection, each experience has shaped me in some way.

But as I look ahead to the next destination, I feel a sense of excitement and anticipation. What adventures await us? What new memories will we make? The possibilities seem endless, and I know that this road trip is just the beginning of an incredible journey.

So, let's keep driving, exploring, and discovering all that this beautiful world has to offer, together. Our family of five.

Hobbies

Hiking boots laced up tight, I hit the trail,
The rustling of leaves and whispering trees,
My mind wanders, thoughts as free as the breeze.
I find peace in the simplicity of hiking,
The beauty of nature, the journey I take,
A moment of escape from the musing of writing.

But when I return home, my mind still writing,
I find solace in the rhythmic hum of my sewing,
The needle and thread gliding the journey I take,
As I create something new from scraps and trees,
A patchwork of colors, a quilt of my hiking,
Each stitch a moment of calm in the bustle of the breeze.

And when my fingers tire of needle and breeze,
I turn to the words, the endless writing,
The flow of thoughts that come with each hike taken,
A story to tell, a memory worth sewing,
A hike through mountains and valleys and trees,
A path to follow, the journey I take.

So whether I'm hiking, sewing, or writing,
Joy is within the trees, the breeze, and the journey I make..

Generational Recipe

In the kitchen's warmth,
Mother's hands work magic spells,
Love in every dish.

In the kitchen's warmth
My children's laughter echoes,
Children play and eat.

In the kitchen's warmth
Chef creates a symphony
Haiku of flavors.

In the kitchen's warmth
Recipes are memories,
Flavors on my tongue.

Recipes passed along,
Flavors never lost.

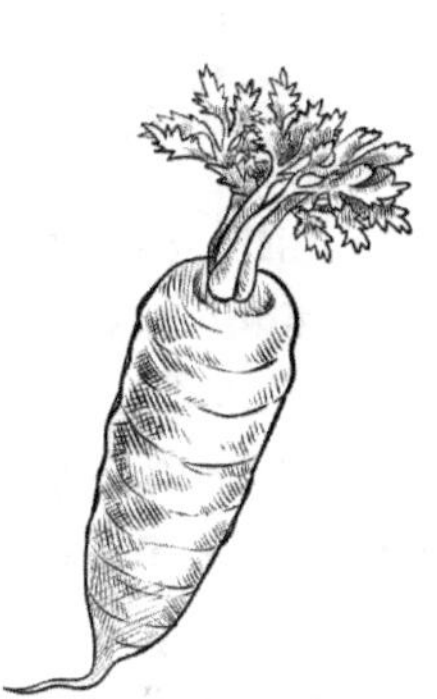

Goodnight

When I was away, I put you to sleep in my
dreams.

My rough tiger with the golden heart that curiously
chases every animal by day was curled up in the
branches up high in a big, branchy tree.

My rainbow haired horse
fell asleep in the flowers.
Amidst the crayons and colors
on paper with dolls and video games.

My little little little,
he snuggles with every blanket
surrounded by the remaining scent
when I last fed you my milk,
always a smile on your face.

My husband,
you fell asleep with a mother's ear,
one always open; but, everything else
was sound asleep.

A Woven Villanelle

Everything relates to everything, they say,
Interconnected, a web we weave,
Intricacies woven every which way.

But how do we decipher the display,
Make sense of the patterns we perceive?
Everything relates to everything, they say.

From atoms small to galaxies at play,
Each piece of the puzzle we receive,
Intricacies woven every which way.

The universe, a grand ballet,
Each step in harmony, never to leave,
Everything relates to everything, they say.

So let us not lose sight, nor betray,
The beauty in the connections we achieve,
Intricacies woven every which way.

For in the end, we are all but clay,
Molded and shaped by what we believe,
Everything relates to everything, they say,
Intricacies woven every which way.

Haikus for
My Green Sewing Friend

My green sewing friend
Threads woven with love and care
Friendship stitched in time

Feeling all fabrics
Thread intertwines, friendship grows
Lunches on weekends

Green hued fabric scraps
Two needles and one thread bind
Long distance friendship

The hum of sewing
A melody of friendship
Fun conversation

With every stitch sewn
A bond between us is formed
Memories take hold

Fabric scraps and dreams
A creative journey shared
My green sewing friend

Freedom to Explore

The wind in my hair, the sun on my skin
The open road stretching out before me
With every mile, a new world begins
The freedom to explore, to be truly free

The open road stretching out before me
A sense of adventure, a thirst for the new
The freedom to explore, to be truly free
My mind wanders,
thoughts drifting like the view

A sense of adventure, a thirst for the new
Memories of the past, hopes for the future
My mind wanders,
thoughts drifting like the view
The beauty of the journey, a constant allure

Memories of the past, hopes for the future
The road ahead, a path to the unknown
The beauty of the journey, a constant allure
The wind in my hair,
the sun on my skin, my only throne.

Your Dreams, My Child

Your dreams are just the beginning, my child,
So, hold them close
and let them guide your way,
For they can take you places that are wild.

The world is yours, so go ahead and be bold,
Don't let anyone tell you
what you can't do today,
Your dreams are just the beginning, my child.

The path you take may not be easy or mild,
But keep pushing forward
and don't be led astray,
For they can take you places that are wild.

Believe in yourself and let your spirit run wild,
And let your heart and soul lead you each day,
Your dreams are just the beginning, my child.

Life may throw you curveballs,
but don't be beguiled,
Just get back up and keep moving,
come what may,
For they can take you places that are wild.

So go forth, my child, and be free all the while,
And know that
your dreams will light up your way,
Your dreams are just the beginning, my child,
For they can take you places that are wild.

My Turn

It's my turn,
To be the mom
I imagined was mine
But more like the one
that I had.

In motherhood,
I find that
I'm all on my own
although everyone
needs my attention

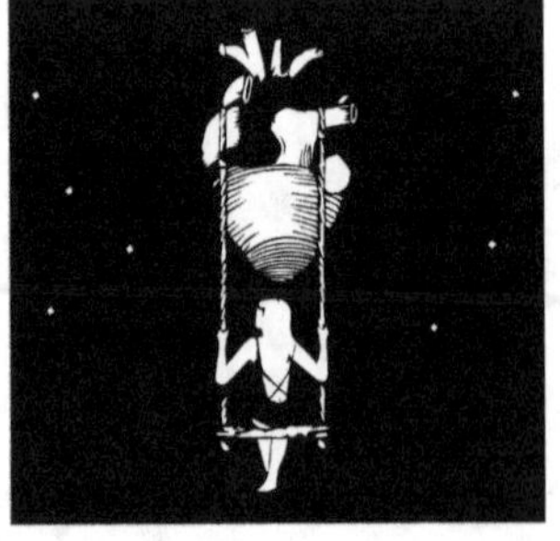

This life
I have chosen
Is mine to create
While days in my past
made me feel limited
by what I was given

I now
Live my life
As a choice
with the benefit
of time on my hands

The lure of money
leads people astray
shortens their days
Whispering noises
reach out to my ear
As they grow louder
It's harder to hear

So, I'll leave that place
to seek my peace.

I find solace
knowing
that I'll hear the words
telling me where to stay.
That place to be
will let me be me.

I'll create my space
and sit on this swing
I'll touch their sweet faces
find comfort within their spaces
knowing that this is all
I ever did need.

Keep Me in this Moment

"Keep me in this moment," I plead,
As time flies by at an alarming rate,
My heart begs for moments to heed.

Memories fade, like a withering seed,
I yearn for moments that don't dissipate,
"Keep me in this moment," I plead.

The future looms, with its unknown breed,
Fears and worries, I cannot abate,
My heart begs for moments to heed.

Every second, a precious deed,
I long to savor, before it's too late,
"Keep me in this moment," I plead.

Life passes by, with its furious speed,
And I'm left to rue moments I cannot recreate,
My heart begs for moments to heed.

So, hold me close, and let me feed,
On every second, before it's too late,
"Keep me in this moment," I plead,
My heart begs for moments to heed.